AF382238

CHOOSING RESILIENCE

Unlocking The Rhythm Of The Human Spirit

JUDENCE KAYITESI

INZOZI PUBLISHER

Content

FOREWORD

December 2023 on a Tuesday morning , I took a spontaneous trip to Ettlingen.

As I sat with Judence Kayitesi at her coffee table watching grey trees outside through the window, we talked about hardships of being a Black woman in Germany. She had experienced discrimination, an unspoken reality of Bipoc (Black Indigenous and People of Color) working in a white dominated environment.

One thing became clear; no matter how hard I tried to distract her from her disappointment I wasn't going to succeed. Maybe because I am not one of those born-qualified motivational speakers. Or maybe because it would be an illusion to ignore a problem that people face on a daily basis because of how they have been born. So, we started talking back about how she survived the Genocide against Tutsi, in 1994. As we went back through her life challenges and how she had managed to go through them and still she is able to laugh and embrace life, her face brightened. Judence looked at me and said " you know what, nothing can actually break me."

There is a way being a genocide survivor will always lead decisions that one makes in life. You know you have to move forward, life goes on no matter what. The way that history of Judence and her past challenges have shaped her resilience is an inspiration for many women.

To each person going through hardships, may this book strengthen your resilience.

With love,

Divine Gashugi, *Author and artistic director*

Chapter I

BRIDGES OF HEARTACHE: A JOURNEY OF LOSS, LOVE AND RENEWAL

In the aftermath of the 1994 genocide against the Tutsi that killed more than a million people, my life took a new turn. After, The Rwanda Patriotic Army (RPA), now Rwanda Patriotic Front (RPF) had ended the genocide against the Tutsi's atrocities, myself, my two brothers and my two-year-old niece, sought to restore our shattered world. Determined to start afresh I wanted to honor the dream of creating my own family that I have always wanted, envisioning to have a maximum of six children.

When I was 21 years old, in 2004, I met a 48 years old man from Germany who was working with a non-profit organization in Rwanda at the time. Despite a significant age gap, we embarked on a journey of companionship, the joyful moments we shared deepened our relationship and committing for a lifetime together was all we wished-for. After 2 years of a great relationship, we exchanged our vows, officially becoming husband and wife.

As life have always its share of challenges, I lost my cousin who succumbed to trauma caused by the atrocities of genocide against the Tutsi, leaving behind a toddler that I officially adopted later for the love I had for children. Having her in our family, with my other two biological sons made motherhood wonderful.

A short time after our wedding we had to relocate to a different country due to my husband's professional commitments, living in Cape Town, South Africa for a year before we moved to Addis Ababa that became our home for the next three years and that is where my two sons were born. In 2010, we had to move again to Europe in Germany because of my husband's new job, where cultural and environment differences brought significant challenges.

Germany brought forth a tapestry of diverse cultures, unlike anything I had experienced before. Adapting to this new way of life became a shared experience for our family.

The age disproportion between my husband and I, took a huge toll on our relationship where misunderstandings rose. Divergent interests and hobbies fueled quiet a new direction that our relationship was taking. Being a genocide against the Tutsi survivor, and him having interests into celebrating Halloween and other triggering activities brought back past wounds and haunting memories of the 1994 Tutsi killings.

In addition to that, I was very shocked to learn that my husband had other children outside our marriage which made our relationship bitter.

At the age of 23, I found myself stepping into the realm of marriage with a man who was almost three time my age which continued to be an obstacle to our marriage despite joyful moments we experienced in the beginning of our relationship. All of this, was happening while I was learning on how to tap into motherhood as well as to become a wife, making it difficult for our family to thrive. In essence, I found myself in a space where I was always comparing myself to my husband who had more experience and maturity considering the age gap between us. The uncertainty grew and I couldn't figure out what I truly wanted out of life.

The fact that I had lost almost all my family members, parents, aunties, uncles and cousins made me lose a part of myself where I wasn't seeing the future the way it was supposed to be. Therefore, asking myself the right questions, I realized that I had to face the reality which hit me in the face like a burst of water, putting me on a self-discovery journey about my identity and what I desired most. It was a moment of awakening for me, steering the possibility of a new life trajectory. Meanwhile, I had started feeling like my husband perceived me as a child who had no dreams and aspirations, where he expected me to stay at home and be content of what he was providing for the family, leading to the fear of spreading my wings and exploring new horizons.

As our relationship continued to become more challenging, both of us took a period of introspection, assessing where things had gone wrong and also thinking of solutions. After, recognizing the growing strain, we decided to temporarily take separate ways.

During our separation, the lack of communication persisted and being the primary caregiver for our children became even more difficult.

Feeling powerless and desperate, we sought assistance from social professionals that provide counselling to families facing domestic problems. The outcome was not helpful as the age difference and cultural diversities continued to be an obstacle to our relationship which also impacted every aspect of our lives.

Despite our best efforts, the chasm between us remained unbridged. Unfortunately, we made the difficult decision to take separate ways permanently, opting for a peaceful separation. Each of us embarked on a journey to start afresh, the legalities of our divorce were finalized in 2019, marking the end of a chapter but also the beginning of a new phase in both our lives.

Ending our marriage was very heartbreaking, taking me back to how I lost my family during the genocide against the Tutsi, as well as remembering how I survived the killer's machetes that left me with severe scars. I just wished that my parents could be there to comfort me and tell me that I was not alone. In that space of wondering, I wished that they would have advised me to marry a younger man of my age, my soul was filled with pain, confusion and regret.

For my children sake, I could not have stayed into that situation, I had to be brave and set a greater example of not being defined by my problems but rather embrace what life has thrown at me and be a caring and nurturing mother they were expecting me to be. Even though we separated, I am grateful for the support my ex-husband continues to provide. His contributions have facilitated my brothers' education in international schools and started their lives in better conditions, and he also supported the education and resettlement of my niece in a promising way. Despite the end of our marriage, we maintained a great co-parenting relationship, working together for the well-being of our children. He remained committed to meet their daily needs and extends a helping hand whenever required.

I am also grateful for the people who supported me during the hard times when we were going through a divorce, so many people have prayed for me, supported me, comfort me, some have even supported me in tangible ways. I don't know where I would be if it wasn't for them. I always pray to God that he blesses them.

Going through a divorce has taught me a few things that I would like to share with couples facing challenges which could end up in a divorce, my advice is to opt for amicable separations and maintain a supportive friendship. It is crucial to prioritize the well-being of the children regardless of differences.

Chapter II

SWEEPING AWAY OBSTACLES: NAVIGATING DISCRIMINATION AND BUILDING RESILIENCE

I used to love studying and believed it was the key to achieving my goals. After losing my parents, neighbors, siblings, aunties, and uncles in the 1994 genocide against Tutsi, I thought education was my way out. I wanted a future free from financial struggles, where I could provide for my kids and brothers. So, I put all my efforts into finding a school or training center to learn skills that would make my dreams become reality.

When we arrived in Germany, my children were very young. Their father wanted me to stay home all the time, and not pursue any of my dreams. My youngest was only six months old when we arrived. I started teaching myself German and occasionally attended a nearby school, but with young kids, my learning time was limited. Though it was not easy for me, I managed to get an A2 grade in my first German language exam.

When my younger children went to nursery school, I also wanted to resume my studies, go to university and get a degree for a better future for myself. Unfortunately, my husband didn't support the idea. Ever since I was a child, I always wanted to become a doctor inspired by my father's and auntie's stomach flu disease. They have gone through painful stomach issues. Therefore, going to medical school would have helped me treat them as well as other members of my family and also my community.

Without my husband's support, I had to find another way. I landed a job as a cleaner at the local university, thinking it could be a stepping stone. I discovered that by attending a cleaning course, I could earn a good salary compared to those without the certification. So, I enrolled in a three-year program to become a certified janitor.

Becoming a janitor, opportunities for me were many, whether it was for being a custodian, cleaner, caretaker or just signing big contracts for buildings and offices maintenance. Being a certified cleaner, I could work for hospitals and residential complexes. I was thrilled to be part of creating safe, clean and comfortable environment for clients.

The profession of a janitor, I had undertaken required a diverse skill set, where I had to be proficient in my cleaning tasks, be able to manage the time well, paying attention to details and also make sure I communicate to my boss and clients effectively. I had to make sure that all spaces were sanitized, remembered to remove all the trashes and also insure clean floors. Despite all my efforts and maintaining professionalism, I encountered racism at work. Being a janitor wasn't enough to be despised by some of white people but also being black was like committing a crime because of the color of my skin.

When I experienced racism, there is no place I could go and report that particular behavior and doing so seemed futile; no one was willing to condemn them.

As I balanced the challenges of being a janitor with the burden of racism, I found myself fighting on two fronts. Cleaning became more than just a job; it became a symbol of resilience. It was my way of silently resisting the discriminatory forces at play. The struggle against racism merged with the challenge for personal and professional growth.

In my first year of learning how to clean where I lived in East Germany. There was a teacher who often made me feel bad about my work. Once, when he asked me to repeat a German word, I said it in a way that wasn't perfect, like a native German speaker. The whole class laughed at me, and I felt really sad. It seemed like they were discriminating against me.

In my second year, another teacher unfairly graded my work. Even though I felt confident about my answers, he always gave me zero grades just because sometimes I mixed some German with a few English words. I had a Russian classmate, who knew less German than me and used more English words compared to me, but he always got good grades. It felt unfair, and I felt discriminated against because of my skin color and where I came from as an African.

However, there was one teacher who encouraged me. He understood that language mistakes didn't matter as much as the content of what I wrote, is in the right way of the subject. He told me to continue working hard, saying that if it was him learning my native language, he couldn't even understand or speak a single word in my native Kinyarwanda. This teacher valued my efforts, encouraged me to put in more effort, and gave me the grades I deserved.

All these experiences were hurtful because I always lost grades not because of wrong answers but because of discrimination.

I remember one morning heading to work, while in the staff van with four of my colleagues including myself, they started smoking despite the fact that it was not allowed to smoke in public or enclosed spaces like in the car, unless every person present would give permission. I overheard them mocking me that I couldn't report them since no one would take me seriously because of the color of my skin, believing that I had no right to speak up in their country.

During work, they treated me poorly, saying I shouldn't be part of their company and should have another job. They avoided me, laughed when I tried to join them, and considered me from a poor country with lack of knowledge. I will not forget when one of my colleagues said that he wondered if we had fridges and stoves in Africa.

Experiencing this particular behavior was painful to me, not only it made the working environment toxic and uncomfortable but also reinforced a sense of isolation and solitude became home. These experiences directed to the need for creating awareness about this issue in order to foster a more inclusive and supportive environment for the black community in Germany.

But amongst all this negativity, there was this one teacher who stood out. This teacher didn't just criticize; instead, he encouraged me to never give up, to push myself, and to work hard. This teacher recognized my intelligence and saw the effort I was putting into learning, quickly grasping the lessons. Unlike others, this teacher couldn't muster the courage to learn English like I did with the German language.

This teacher instilled confidence in me and even went out of their way to advocate for my abilities to other teachers. They saw me as a good student, and this support played a significant role in my achieving success in my studies. It's a reminder that, despite the discrimination and challenges, some see your potential and push you to rise above the prejudices.

The journey from tragedy to triumph, from self-study to janitorial certification, is a testament to the human spirit's indomitable nature. It's a story of overcoming adversity, where education and career growth intersect with the harsh realities of racial discrimination. I became a janitor not just to clean buildings but to clean away biases, proving that strength can emerge even in the face of the deepest societal prejudices.

The pivotal chapter in my life unfolded in the aftershock of my separation from my husband. The idea of finding a new place to call home seemed like a straightforward endeavor, sustained by the assurance of financial stability. Little did I know that the journey ahead would be perforated with unforeseen complexities, unveiling the harsh realities of the housing market and the lingering specter of racial bias.

Among the disturbances of my personal life, I found myself seeking refuge in what the Germans appropriately term Frauenhaus, which means women's shelter. These shelters, intricately designed to be a haven for women facing an array of challenges, provide not just physical accommodation but also crucial emotional and legal support. Whether grappling with the aftermath of domestic violence, abuse, or the upheaval of separation and divorce, Frauenhaus aims to offer a secure and supportive environment.

My attempt to navigate the intricacies of the rental market took an unexpected turn when I enlisted the help of a German friend to secure a house. The initial promise of a smooth transaction was shattered when we encountered the property owner in person. The abrupt change in the owner's demeanor, evident as he laid eyes on my blackness, left me stunned. In a matter of minutes, the house that was ostensibly available just moments ago had miraculously found another tenant, leaving me to grapple with the bitter realization that racial bias was an insidious obstacle in my pursuit of a stable residence.

The emotional toll of this encounter was profound. As a black woman in a foreign land, I found myself pondering the broader implications of this discrimination. How could I build a life in a country where every step forward seemed hindered by the color of my skin? The bitterness of such experiences lingered as a constant companion, a reminder that, despite my efforts, my very existence was met with unjustified hostility.

This ordeal was particularly distressing when considering the larger narrative of my life. Having left my home country in 2006, traversing various African nations due to the requirements of my ex-husband's job, I found myself bereft of familial support. The 1994 genocide against the Tutsi had claimed the lives of the majority of my family members, leaving me with only a few connections, including my niece and an aunt. In the absence of a familial safety net, the desire for stability and a place to call my own became an unwavering beacon.

Returning to the apartment I once shared with ex-husband, the dichotomy of my existence became stark. On one hand, I was a mother with children of German blood and ancestry, and on the other, we were subjected to discrimination that stemmed from our African heritage. The irony was palpable, the very essence of my children, their unique blend of African and German identities, became a source of discrimination.

In the face of adversity, my children's father emerged as a beacon of support. Realizing what we were going through, the children and I, my ex-husband suggested that we could return to the familiar confines of our previous apartment. While he embarked on the seemingly straightforward task of securing a new residence, I found myself entangled in a protracted, four-month struggle to find a place I could call home. The bitter taste of racism lingered; a constant reminder of the hurdles I faced solely based on the color of my skin.

My return to the apartment, while providing a semblance of stability, triggered a deep reflection on the trajectory of my life. Cleaning spaces as a janitor no longer resonated with the vision, I had for myself and my children. In pursuit of healing and personal growth, I sought the guidance of a professional therapist. This transformative journey, guided by therapeutic intervention, led me to the realization that my experiences held the potential for profound storytelling. From the depths of my struggles, the idea to chronicle my journey took shape. The result was my first book, "A Broken Life," a testament to the resilience of the human spirit in the face of adversity.

It marked the inception of a new chapter in my life, one fueled by the desire not just to overcome my challenges but to inspire others facing similar struggles.

Emboldened by this newfound purpose, I resolved to deepen my integration into German society. The language, a gateway to cultural understanding, became my focus. Progressing from a basic A2 proficiency to a more nuanced B1 level, I recognized the importance of a holistic understanding of the culture that now enveloped me.

As my language skills evolved, so did my aspirations. The notion of becoming a teacher for young children in nursery schools took root. The decision was multifaceted a mission for personal stability, a desire to immerse myself in German culture, and a commitment to shaping the future by educating the youngest members of the society. It was a deliberate choice to understand German society from its foundational roots, mirroring the progression of a child through stages of development.

Embarking on a three-year journey of teaching courses, I found fulfillment in nurturing and educating children under the age of six. The classroom became a canvas where I painted not just the brushstrokes of academic learning but also the nuances of cultural understanding. The children under my care, with their innocent curiosity, became my allies in this journey of mutual learning.

The decision to deviate from my initial dream of becoming a doctor in medicine was not without a hint of regret. The challenges I faced, both racially and circumstantially, altered the trajectory of my ambitions. Yet, in the role of a teacher, I discovered a profound sense of purpose. The dream of healing, although in a different form, found expression in shaping young minds and hearts.

The discrimination that had marked my early struggles began to dissipate in the warm embrace of my chosen vocation. As a teacher in Germany, I found a sense of belonging that transcended the barriers of race and ethnicity. My children, once subjected to the stigma of being labeled "African" in their country of origin, now thrived in an environment where their mother, rooted in both African and German cultures, played a pivotal role in shaping their understanding of identity and values.

I remember sitting in the living room with my son, asking me the reason why Tutsi were killed in the 1994 genocide against the Tutsi, supposing that they might have done something wrong in their community. Responding, I returned him similar question asking him why white people hated black and mixed people. He took a moment and told me that he grasped my message to him. When figured out the answer by himself, I realized how much he has grown up and tapping into the sense of thriving in a midst of a chaotic culture.

Reflecting on this journey, the struggles, discrimination, and triumphs, I am reminded of the resilience of the human spirit. The path I tread was fraught with challenges, but through unwavering focus, hard work, and a persistent belief that every adversity could be overcome, I emerged not just as a survivor but as a triumphant individual.

To those facing their trials, I extend a resounding message of encouragement; stay focused, work diligently, and play hard. The road may be difficult, but with unwavering determination, everything will eventually fall into place. My story is a testament to the transformative power of resilience, a beacon of hope for those navigating the labyrinth of life's challenges.

Chapter III

EMBRACING THE UNSEEN: A SYMPHONY OF STRENGTH AND TRIUMPH

In the intricate tapestry of life, where threads of joy and sorrow interweave, I found myself navigating a path fraught with unseen perils. It was a journey marked by the silent struggle of an invisible illness; a battle fought within the confines of my own body. As I reflect upon the chapters of my life, I am drawn back to the canvas of my youth, a time when innocence clashed with the harsh realities of a body harboring secrets.

In the uncontrolled age of puberty, when my peers reveled in the simplicity of their menstrual cycles, I stood on the edge of normality, grappling with a condition both mysterious and frightening. Each monthly visitation of my cycle was accompanied by a descent into the abyss of ill health. Various symptoms overwhelmed me, debilitating illness, a critical three-day period of suffering, and a relentless rejection of sustenance that rendered even the mere act of swallowing a tough task. My sanctuary became the sterile walls of a hospital room, where the only respite came in the form of normal saline, commonly known as serum, coursing through my veins. In those moments of illness, the very essence of nourishment became challenging, as every time I wanted to eat or drink something, I could not keep it because I always ended up vomiting.

The suffering extended beyond the physical realm, manifesting in dangerous abdominal pain that contorted my body in silent screams. A torrent of blood accompanied each cycle, leaving me drained and fragile. The ache extended to the depths of my back, a constant reminder that my body was a battleground where pain waged an unrelenting war.

Yet, in the ignorance of youth, the notion of seeking help in the office of a gynecologist escaped me, and I resigned myself to endure this storm alone.

It was only in the melting pot of South Africa, after embarking on the journey of marriage and pregnancy, that the curtain of ignorance began to lift. A visit to the gynecologist, punctuated by the stark illumination of an ultrasound screen, revealed the existence of myomas within my uterus. At the time, I learned that myomas also known as uterine fibroids, were noncancerous growths that take root during a woman's childbearing years. Composed of smooth muscle cells and fibrous tissue, these enigmatic tumors can incite a myriad of symptoms, heightened menstrual flow, pelvic pain, frequent urination, backaches, and discomfort during intimacy. While the origin of these growths remains mysterious, a complex interplay of genetics and hormonal imbalances is often implicated.

As the doctor unraveled the enigma that had haunted me since adolescence, the gravity of the situation was underscored by the heart-wrenching news of a miscarriage and the cruel theft of my first pregnancy. In spite of being anxious with pain and loss, God blessed me with the arrival of my first two sons in 2008 and 2009. However, the dream of a larger family, an aspiration that emerged from the depths of my heart as a salve for the wounds inflicted by the 1994 genocide against the Tutsi, began to unravel among the complexities of familial aspirations and undisclosed progeny.

In the crucible of misunderstanding and unmet expectations, my marriage ended, leaving me to cope not only with the scars of emotional turmoil but also with a body burdened by complications. The worry of endometriosis, a terrible illness in my reproductive health, descended upon me. This sneaky illness, was an abnormal growth of tissue on the lining of my uterus outside its natural confines, resulting in severe pelvic pain and hindering fertility. Medical researchers suggested that there was no cure to my condition, even though its symptoms could be alleviated through medication or surgery and this idea terrified me.

Enduring the unbearable pain, I underwent three surgeries with the hope of getting relief, only to find myself again in the clutches of persistent affliction.

A new chapter unfolded with the arrival of a compassionate man, a beacon of love amid my storm-ridden life. United by a shared understanding and a reservoir of unwavering love, we embarked on the journey of creating a family. Yet, the cruel hand of fate dictated otherwise, orchestrating three heart-wrenching miscarriages and the unyielding growth of myomas. The somber realization dawned, there was no alternative but to part ways with my uterus.

In the cold clinical manner of the doctor's words, the gravity of the decision echoed through the corridors of my consciousness. The prognosis was stark, emphasizing the precarious nature of a continued pursuit of motherhood. The echoes of cultural stigmas reverberated through my mind, conjuring visions of societal judgments on women without a uterus, reduced to a mere semblance of their gender and even raised a man's voice. The specter of cancer loomed ominously, casting shadows over any lingering hopes.

Amidst the labyrinth of choices, I pleaded for a reprieve, a chance to try once more before surrendering to the inevitable. The request was reluctantly accepted, my uterus would be relinquished at the age of 39, a scary concession to the relentless march of time and the demands of my health. The surgery, a final act of liberation from the shackles of pain, marked the end of an era defined by reproductive struggles.

There was a time, in the depths of my ignorance, I believed the uterus was the same as a woman's heart. In my uninformed perception, I thought that its removal equated to the termination of life for a girl or woman. The terror struck me when the doctor uttered those fateful words; my uterus had been removed. It felt like the end of the world, a crushing blow to my existence.

As I was grappling with the news, I discovered that I was not alone in this ordeal. Friends, other women who had faced the similar challenge, became my beacon of hope. They shared their stories of resilience and triumph, dismantling my preconceived notion that life without a uterus was synonymous with failure. Instead, they were living proof that one could thrive beyond such setbacks.

With fear, I recounted my tale to these resilient women, expecting shame but I received wisdom. "Don't panic," they advised, "your life is far from over. Losing your uterus may alter some of your plans, especially those involving expanding your family, but it doesn't mean your dreams are shattered." Their words resonated like a healing balm, soothing my fears and reinforcing my perspective.

These remarkable women taught me a valuable lesson; even though a woman possesses a uterus, various factors can contribute to challenges in realizing her maternal aspirations. Fertility is a complex interplay of physical, emotional, and environmental factors. Medical conditions, such as polycystic ovary syndrome, endometriosis, or uterine abnormalities, can affect fertility. Hormonal imbalances, irregular ovulation, or issues with ovum quality may also pose challenges.

Beyond the physical aspects, emotional and psychological factors play a significant role. Stress, anxiety, and lifestyle factors can impact fertility. Moreover, relationships, societal expectations, and personal circumstances may create additional complexities.

In essence, the ability to conceive and bear children is a multifaceted process, and the presence of a uterus is just one piece of the puzzle. Recognizing the diverse challenges that women may face on their journey to motherhood fosters a more comprehensive understanding of the complexities involved.

Life is full of unforeseen challenges, they continue, and sometimes, we lose things we hold dear. But it's crucial to accept the changes, adapt, and trust that God will grant you the strength to navigate new paths." Their stories became a testament to the power of acceptance and resilience.

They illustrated their point with their own lives. Look at us, they urged, we are content, our projects are flourishing, and we've overcome the obstacles life put our way. You, too, can emerge victorious. Accept what you cannot change, move forward, and believe that everything will eventually fall into place. Sooner or later, you'll find gratitude in your heart for the journey you've traveled.

Their counsel became a guiding light in my darkest hours. Today, I stand as a testament to their words. Happiness pervades every facet of my life, and I harbor no resentment. Instead, I find comfort in expressing gratitude for the blessings given to me by a benevolent God.

To those facing hardships, whether is sickness, disappointments, discrimination or failures, I extend the lessons I have learned.

The journey of this life is a ride you cannot control, a series of challenges that mold us into unshakable individuals. Strength arises from navigating tough situations, and in the crucible of adversity, we forge resilience.

So, I implore everyone facing trials to embrace prayer, hard work, self-belief, focus, and patience. These virtues, when woven into the fabric of your existence, will carry you through the storm. Believe that you are capable of overcoming anything, and with time, you will achieve more than you ever thought possible.

The echoes of my journey, a symphony of pain and resilience, reverberate in the written word. It is within the crucible of suffering that the seed of inspiration germinated, compelling me to pen words of encouragement for those who may be walking similar paths. The indomitable human spirit, fortified by faith and resilience, emerged as the theme of my narrative, a testament to the enduring power of hope in the face of adversity.

In the tapestry of my life, a steadfast companion emerged a man whose unwavering love and support weathered the storms of sickness and depression. In his eyes, I found support and acceptance, a refuge from the societal judgments that sought to define my worth by the presence or absence of a uterus. "It's okay," he whispered in moments of despair, "our love transcends the confines of biology. Be strong, be happy, for God is in control of everything."

The chorus of support extended beyond the confines of a romantic relationship, echoing in the unwavering solidarity of my children, friends, and family. Their presence, an immeasurable source of strength, became a great source of hope and healing for my faltering spirit. As I was standing at the precipice of enjoyment in life, a man breathed life into my darkest days, and I found myself ornamented with the covering of serenity.

Today, I am a mother of three, a testament to the resilience of the human spirit and the capacity of love to forge bonds beyond the biological. My two biological sons and an adopted daughter are the embodiments of a newfound joy, a resounding affirmation that life, in its myriad complexities, can still offer solace and fulfillment. Gratitude dwells within me, a river that flows in appreciation of my new companion, my children, my family and my friends who stood unwavering in the tempest of my tribulations, after separating from my ex-husband.

As the sun sets on the landscape of my tumultuous journey, I cast my gaze towards the horizon with a heart brimming with gratitude. Through the labyrinth of pain and loss, I have emerged not as a victim of circumstance, but as a testament to the transformative power of resilience and unwavering hope. Today, I celebrate not only the passage of time but the triumph of the human spirit, a symphony that continues to play, resonating with the echoes of a life lived in defiance of the shadows that sought to surround it.

In conclusion, my story is not one of despair but of triumph over adversity. It is a testament to the human spirit's resilience, the ability to rise above circumstances and emerge stronger. Life's challenges, no matter how frightening, can be navigated with grace, faith, and an unwavering belief in oneself.

Chapter IV

OVERCOMING AND ACHIEVING: RESULT OF PERSISTENCE AND TRANSFORMATION

As the pages of my life continue to turn, the chapters that unfold reveal a narrative of triumph over adversity. It's a story of tenacity, resilience, and a journey that, against all odds, leads to success. This journey wasn't a stroll down an easy path; it was a climb up a rugged mountain, each step fraught with challenges and obstacles. The pinnacle of this climb, however, brings me to a vantage point where the view is breathtaking, and the air is filled with the sweet scent of accomplishment.

The genesis of this transformation comes from a commitment I made to myself, a commitment to financial stability, independence, and the pursuit of dreams that once seemed unattainable. Saving money became not just a habit but a ritual, a conscious effort to secure a with financial stability that will free us from the shackles of mental struggles and discriminatory hurdles. I would allocate a portion of every hard-earned coin to a savings account, nurturing a seed that would eventually sprout into the tree of financial freedom.

The struggles mentioned in the preceding chapters were not merely words on a page; they were the battles fought in the channels of real life. Discrimination, particularly when seeking housing, was a terrible opponent. The journey involved facing biases, navigating through bureaucratic mazes, and confronting a system that sometimes seemed designed to prevent progress. Despite these challenges, the flame of determination burned bright within me, pushing me forward when the road seemed impassable.

The savings weren't just a store of money; they were a testament to discipline, sacrifice, and a vision for the future. Each coin accurately saved brought me a step closer to a dream that had been imprinted in the depths of my heart, the dream of owning my own house. The significance of this dream wasn't merely in the possession of a property; it was a symbol of breaking free from the cycle of uncertainty and establishing a stronghold of stability for myself and my family.

As I stand on the edge of this dream, the savings clock in at an impressive 90%. The finish line is in sight, and the remaining 10% is more a formality than a challenge. The satisfaction that accompanies this financial milestone is profound. It's the peak of years of disciplined financial planning, a journey that transformed me from someone who struggled to make ends meet to a person who can confidently say; I am financially stable.

However, financial stability isn't just about accumulating wealth; it's about wielding the power to tackle any unforeseen circumstance that life may throw my way. It's about providing my children with more than just the basics; it's about affording them opportunities to explore the world, experience different cultures, and broaden their horizons. Family vacations, once a distant luxury, are now a reality, and I am humbled and grateful for every moment spent creating memories with my loved ones.

In the course of this journey, I have come to appreciate the significance of money management and the importance of imparting these values to others. To those who are still navigating the labyrinth of financial uncertainties, I offer a piece of advice born from personal experience. It's not just about saving for the sake of saving; it's about having a purpose behind every money saved. Write down your plans, articulate your dreams, and let your savings be the fuel that pushes you toward those aspirations.

The transformation from a struggling individual to a woman of values has not only been a personal achievement but has also reaped recognition from the German society that I now call home.

The challenges faced, the battles won, and the ultimate position as a teacher for young children stand as a testament to the belief society has placed in me.

Teaching, particularly in the formative years of a child's life, is a responsibility I carry with a profound sense of honor. The importance of these early years in shaping the future of a nation cannot be overstated. It's during this time that children absorb the very essence of a culture, learn the do's and don'ts of society, grasp the details of language and communication, and develop the foundational skills that will serve them in their future educational endeavors.

Taking care of the nation's children, especially in a foreign land, is not just a job; it's a treasured achievement. The parents who entrust their little ones to my care, and the leaders of the school who have faith in my ability to contribute to the foundation of these young minds, have given me a responsibility that goes beyond the classroom.

The gratitude I feel is immeasurable. Society, which once may have overlooked or discriminated against me, now recognizes the value I bring. I have become not just a teacher but an inspiration of hope for those who, like me, have faced hardships and emerged victorious. The narrative has shifted from one of struggle to one of success, and as I stand at the intersection of dreams fulfilled and new horizons, I am a living testament to the transformative power of perseverance and disciplined financial planning.

For anyone willing to achieve success, I encourage you to learn about how money works. If you can earn even a modest income, cultivate the habit of saving with a purpose. Save with a plan of how the money will be used and let every coin have a designated role in shaping your future. The journey may be challenging, but the destination is worth every sacrifice.

As a child growing up in the lush landscapes of Rwanda, surrounded by the majestic hills and vibrant cultures of East Africa, the art of storytelling was woven into the very fabric of my existence. The evenings were adorned with tales of heroes and heroines, folklore that danced on the edges of reality, and myths that echoed through generations. It was a tradition passed down orally, a symphony of words that painted intense pictures in the minds of those who listened. These stories were the bedrock of our identity, the mortar that held together the bricks of our cultural heritage.

However, as I delved into the world of literature and expanded my horizons, I began to recognize the transformative power that written words held. In Germany, where I found myself surrounded by a different cultural tapestry, I witnessed the daily ritual of parents reading to their children.

It was a practice embedded in their lifestyle, an investment in the intellectual and emotional growth of the next generation. Books became a gateway to knowledge, a vessel through which stories, lessons, and dreams were passed on.

The stark contrast between the reading habits in Germany and those in Rwanda Surprised me. In my homeland, stories were often spoken, shared, and remembered, but the written word struggled to find its place in the hearts of the people. The power of literature, the magic that unfolded when words were carefully captured and preserved, was a treasure waiting to be unearthed.

The realization of this disparity struck me even more forcefully when I completed my first book. Eager to share my creation with the world, I ventured into the dominion of publishers, seeking a partner to bring my vision to life. However, each encounter with established publishing houses left me disheartened. Every entity I approached sought to mold my work according to their commercial interests, to edit it in ways that compromised the authenticity of my message. It became evident that the path to publishing was fraught with compromises, where the author's voice often became a casualty of profit margins.

Fueled by a determination to preserve the integrity of my work and inspired by the untapped potential in the African literary landscape, the idea of creating my own publishing house began to germinate. The seed of Inzozi Publishers was planted, and its roots delved deep into the soil of my aspirations. Inzozi, a word in Kinyarwanda, a mother tongue meaning "dreams", that resonates with the very essence of dreaming, became the guiding star for this venture.

Inzozi Publishers emerged as an independent publishing company in 2023, with its foundations firmly rooted in Germany. The aim was clear; to create a space where African writers, particularly those from Rwanda, could flourish without compromising their artistic vision. The scope of Inzozi Publishers extended across a diverse spectrum of literary genres, embracing literature, non-fiction, novels, memoirs, research, and journals. We envisioned a platform where stories could be told in innovative and creative ways, and where the authentic voices of African authors could reverberate. The heartbeat of Inzozi Publishers resonates with the conviction that memory is a sacred vessel.

We recognized the need to preserve the stories that define us, and this commitment found expression in our emphasis on publishing research and memoirs related to the last genocide of the 20th century; the 1994 Genocide against

Tutsi in Rwanda. Beyond the darkness of that tragic chapter, we sought to illuminate the stories of resilience, reconstruction, and the indomitable spirit of the Rwandan people.

Pan-Africanism became a cornerstone of Inzozi Publishers' philosophy. We passionately believed in promoting stories about Africa by African writers. Our continent is a tapestry of diverse histories, cultures, lifestyles, ecosystems, and life stories, each thread contributing to the rich narrative that is Africa. Inzozi Publishers committed itself to publishing memoirs, histories, cultural narratives, and lifestyle books that showcase the innumerable types of the African experience.

For African writers, whether residing on the continent or scattered across the global diaspora, Inzozi Publishers became an ideal of support. We understood the challenges they faced; the hurdles in accessing reliable publishing opportunities, and the struggle to have their voices heard. Inzozi Publishers pledged to stand by these writers, ensuring that their book ideas underwent comprehensive project development and production, culminating in the realization of their dreams on bookstore shelves worldwide.

As the founder, I harbored a deep hope that this project would be a catalyst for change; not just in the literary landscape but in the very culture of reading in Africa. By making books more accessible, by providing a platform for writers to share their stories, I aspired to instill a love for reading that went beyond borders. Inzozi Publishers isn't merely about publishing; it is about nurturing a cultural shift and encouraging a renaissance in African literature.

In this vision, Inzozi Publishers is not just a publisher; it is a realized dream. It is a commitment to the past, an ode to the resilience of a people, and a guiding light for the future of African literature. It stands as a testament to the belief that stories have the power to bridge gaps, inspire change, and preserve the multifaceted heritage of Africa for generations yet unborn. Inzozi Publishers is more than an imprint on the spine of a book; it is the ink that inscribes dreams onto the pages of reality.

Chapter V

THRIVING AGAINST THE ODDS: A GUIDE TO PERSONAL AND PROFESSIONAL GROWTH

In this particular chapter, I am going to share with you, if not instilling, a long term plan that I developed which will help you to achieve success, involving self-reflection, setting SMART goals (Specific, Measurable, Achievable, Relevant and Time-bound), investing in education and skills, building a support network, prioritizing financial stability, embracing resilience, and practicing self-care. Through these steps, you can pave the way for a future filled with solutions, personal growth, and happiness despite the challenges you face.

Let's go in deep for each point involved:

1. Develop a Positive Mindset

Life can be undeniably challenging, especially for those who find themselves without parents, education, support, or apparent talents. Yet, within the depths of hardship lies the opportunity to shape a positive mindset that can serve as a guiding light toward a better future.

Let's start with a fundamental principle; self-compassion, Life gave me a tough hand, and it's okay to acknowledge that; you might say to yourself. Recognize that circumstances beyond your control don't warrant self-blame. Instead, treat yourself with the kindness and understanding that you deserve to celebrate every small step towards a victory.

Even amidst the most challenging times, there is always something to be grateful for. Today, it could be the air I breathe, the warmth of sunlight or The chance for new beginnings. By consciously focusing on the positive aspects of life, regardless of how small or big they may seem, you can gradually shift your perspective.

While you may lack a high-level education or extraordinary talents, setting realistic goals can provide a sense of purpose. Each accomplishment, no matter how small, contributed to my journey toward a better future. Remember, the journey may be slow, but it is the progress that matters.

Life is bound to throw challenges your way, but it's essential to view setbacks as opportunities for growth. Every failure is a lesson, not a verdict. Learn and grow from every experience, using them as stepping stones toward resilience and wisdom.

Despite the absence of immediate familial support, you have the power to surround yourself with positivity. Engage with uplifting books, motivational speakers, or supportive online communities. Choose to immerse yourself in environments that fuel your optimism and encourage personal development.

Mindfulness is a powerful tool for cultivating positivity. Being present in the moment allows me to appreciate the small joys in life. By distancing yourself from negative thoughts about the past or fears of the future, you create room for positivity to flourish.

Recognizing that your biological family may not be present doesn't mean you have to face life alone. Build a support network by connecting with others who share similar struggles or interests. Sometimes, a kind word or gesture from a friend can make a world of difference.

You may not possess special talents, but you can adopt a growth mindset. See challenges as opportunities for improvement rather than insurmountable obstacles. Dedicate yourself to learning new skills and embrace the belief that your abilities can evolve through effort and perseverance.

Visualizing success is a powerful motivator. Despite my current circumstances, I can picture a brighter future. This mental image will serve as a compass, guiding you toward positive outcomes and reinforcing the belief that your aspirations are within reach.

Lastly, celebrate every small win. Every achievement, no matter how minor, deserves recognition. By acknowledging and appreciating your progress, you reinforce a positive mindset that will carry you through the challenges of life with resilience, hope, and the assurance that a better future is indeed possible.

2. Set Realistic Goals

In life, we often encounter situations that seem insurmountable, challenges that test the very core of our being. If you find yourself grappling with the loss of loved ones, a lack of formal education, and an absence of support, it's essential to recognize the power you possess to shape your destiny. I understand that life has dealt me a difficult hand; you might say. But I am not defined by my circumstances. I have the power to shape my destiny.

Begin by conducting an honest self-assessment. Acknowledge your current situation with clarity and directness. Speak to yourself: I have experienced immense loss, and lack a formal education and support network. But I am not powerless. I can chart a course towards a better future.

Now, let's talk about setting realistic goals. It's crucial to break down your overarching objectives into manageable tasks. Directly address yourself, saying, that while acquiring a high-level education may seem challenging, you can set realistic goals to enhance my skills. I will start with small, achievable milestones, such as enrolling in online courses or seeking vocational training.

Maintain a positive mindset throughout this journey. Speak to yourself affirmatively: I may not have inherited properties, but I can work towards financial stability. I can explore opportunities for employment or entrepreneurship, starting small and gradually expanding my horizons.

Every achievement, no matter how small, is a victory. Celebrate these victories, and let them fuel your motivation for the journey ahead. Directly address your successes: I am proud of the progress I've made. Each achievement is a testament to my strength and determination.

Flexibility is key. Life is unpredictable, and challenges may arise. Directly address the need for adaptability: If one path is blocked, I will explore alternative routes to reach my goals. I am resilient, and I can navigate through uncertainty.

Remember, seeking support is not a sign of weakness but a strength. Directly addressing the importance of a support system, affirms, that while I may not have immediate family or relatives, I can actively build a network of friends, mentors, or like-minded individuals who can offer guidance and encouragement. Together, we can uplift each other.

In conclusion, setting realistic goals through direct speech is a transformative process. It empowers you to confront your reality, outline achievable objectives, maintain a positive mindset, celebrate victories, adapt to change, and seek support. By articulating your aspirations directly, cultivate a resilient spirit that will propel you towards a future filled with solutions and a happy life.

3. Educational Opportunities

In the journey through life, we often encounter challenges that seem insurmountable. For those among us who have lost parents, relatives, and siblings, and find themselves without the privileges of high-level education, properties, or special talents, the path forward may appear obscured. However, it's crucial to recognize that even in the darkest of times, educational opportunities can be the beacon that guides us toward a brighter future.

Let's delve into the transformative power of education, starting with online platforms. In this digital age, knowledge is at our fingertips, accessible with just a click. Many platforms offer courses spanning various subjects. These online courses are not only affordable but often free, enabling individuals to acquire knowledge at their own pace and from the comfort of their surroundings.

Consider exploring community colleges and vocational training centers as well. These institutions provide practical, skill-oriented programs that can equip you with the tools needed for specific industries. Vocational training, in particular, can pave the way for stable employment opportunities, offering a tangible sense of achievement.

Remember, seeking support is not a sign of weakness but a courageous step towards a better future. Reach out to nonprofit organizations, charities, and community groups that extend a helping hand to those yearning for educational opportunities. Scholarships, mentorship programs, and access to essential resources can often be found through these opportunities.

Direct speech is your ally in this journey. When reaching out to educational institutions, mentors, or support organizations, articulate your aspirations and challenges with determination. Speak about your desire for education as a means to break the cycle of adversity, emphasizing how learning can empower you to contribute meaningfully to society.

Networking plays a pivotal role in opening doors to educational opportunities. Attend local community events, workshops, and seminars to connect with professionals and educators who may offer guidance and insights into available resources. Establishing connections within the community can lead to mentorship opportunities, job referrals, and access to educational programs that might not be widely advertised.

Utilize government initiatives and aid programs as well. Many countries have schemes supporting education, ranging from grants and scholarships to low-interest student loans. Research and apply for these programs to alleviate the financial burden associated with pursuing education, allowing you to focus on building a solid academic foundation.

In conclusion, despite facing adversity, educational opportunities abound. Through online platforms, community colleges, support networks, direct speech, networking, and government initiatives, you can chart a course toward a promising future. Education possesses the transformative power to instill confidence, cultivate skills, and open doors to a realm of possibilities, serving as a beacon of hope amidst life's challenges.

4. Build a Support System

In the face of challenging times, when life seems to have dealt its toughest blows, one of the most powerful tools at your disposal is the ability to build a robust support system. Let's explore a variety of strategies and steps that you, as someone navigating difficult circumstances, can take to build a network that uplifts and propels you towards a brighter future.

First and foremost, identify potential supporters in your life. These could be friends, colleagues, or even acquaintances. Reach out to them with a genuine and honest expression of your struggles. I've been going through some tough times, and I value your friendship. Can we talk about what I'm going through?

Mentorship is a powerful resource, especially when facing challenges without a strong educational background. Seek out mentors who can guide you, offering insights and wisdom gained through their experiences. I admire your achievements and would love to learn from your experiences. Can we meet for coffee, and could you share some insights with me?

Consider joining supportive communities, either locally or online, that align with your interests or goals. Engaging with like-minded individuals fosters a sense of belonging and encouragement. I've recently joined this community where people support each other through challenges. It's been really helpful, and I thought you might find it beneficial too.

Don't underestimate the power of professional connections. Networking isn't just about advancing your career; it can also be a source of support. Attend events or conferences related to your interests and forge connections with professionals who may offer guidance. I'm trying to navigate my career path, and I heard you have a wealth of experience. Would you mind if I ask for some advice on how to proceed?

In the digital age, leverage online platforms and resources to connect with individuals who have faced similar circumstances. Social media, forums, and support groups can be invaluable in providing virtual support and a sense of community. I've found some online forums where people share their stories and support each other. It might be helpful for you too.

Consider attending workshops or therapy sessions focused on personal development and coping strategies. These settings provide not only professional guidance but also the opportunity to connect with others facing similar challenges. I've started attending these workshops that focus on building resilience. It's been an eye-opening experience, and I think it could benefit you as well.

Remember, building a support system is a two-way street. Be open to offering support to others, even if it's just lending a listening ear. Reciprocal relationships strengthen connections and create a more supportive environment. I appreciate your support, and I want you to know that I'm here for you too. If you ever need someone to talk to, I'm just a call away.

In conclusion, building a support system is not just a necessity; it's a lifeline. Through reaching out to others, fostering connections, and being open to both giving and receiving support, you can cultivate a network that provides emotional, professional, and practical assistance. This, will eventually contribute to a more fulfilling and hopeful life, even in the face of seemingly insurmountable challenges.

5. Explore Employment Opportunities

In the journey of overcoming profound adversity, the pursuit of employment opportunities emerges as a pivotal lifeline. Imagine someone, a resilient soul, who has faced profound loss, lacks a high-level education, possesses no significant assets, and finds themselves without a support system. These individual dreams of a brighter future, are full of solutions and happiness, yet the path forward appears daunting. In such times, exploring employment opportunities becomes not just a means of sustenance but a transformative force for change.

Imagine yourself, as a determined individual, standing at the crossroads of hardship and hope. The first step is to recognize your inherent worth and the untapped potential within you. Speak directly to yourself; acknowledge your strengths, skills, and passions. Remember, employment opportunities are not confined to formal education or material possessions; they often hinge on your ability to adapt, learn, and contribute.

In the realm of employment, experience holds substantial weight. In interviews, address potential employers directly and share personal narratives that showcase your resilience, problem-solving skills, and strong work ethic in the face of personal challenges. Let your story be a testament to your ability to navigate adversity and emerge stronger on the other side.

Networking is a game-changer. Address professionals directly, attend job fairs, and utilize online platforms like LinkedIn. Speak to potential mentors or industry experts, expressing your eagerness to learn and contribute. Emphasize your commitment to personal growth and professional development.

Volunteering is a powerful strategy. Directly approach organizations aligned with your interests, offering your time and skills in exchange for valuable experience. This not only adds substance to your resume but establishes meaningful connections within the industry.

Continuous learning is indispensable. Address educational institutions, online platforms, or vocational training centers directly. Express your eagerness to acquire new skills and enhance existing ones. Showcase a commitment to self-improvement, making yourself more appealing to potential employers seeking individuals with a growth mindset.

Perseverance is your secret weapon. Address yourself with unwavering determination. Emphasize your tenacity, conveying that you are not defined by past hardships but motivated to create a better future. Employers value resilience and a positive attitude as essential qualities in potential candidates.

In conclusion, the pursuit of employment opportunities is a multifaceted journey, requiring self-assessment, networking, volunteering, continuous learning, and unwavering perseverance. As you navigate this path, remember that you are not alone, and also put in mind this; Tough times never last, but tough people do. By adopting a proactive and direct approach, you can transcend your circumstances, paving the way toward a future filled with solutions and the happiness you envision.

6. Financial Planning

In the wake of life-altering tragedies, building a financial foundation becomes more than just a practical necessity; it transforms into a beacon of hope, guiding the way toward a future filled with solutions and happiness. Picture yourself in a conversation with a wise advisor, one who understands your struggle and is determined to help you transcend the challenges that life has thrown your way. Here's a roadmap to financial recovery and resilience, conveyed in direct speech as if this sage mentor is speaking directly to you, the resilient individual facing seemingly insurmountable odds.

Let's start by facing the stark reality together. Take a moment to understand your current financial standing. List your sources of income and examine your essential expenses. This is your starting point, and no matter how bleak it may seem, acknowledging where you are sets the stage for progress.

As you outline your monthly expenses, be brutally honest with yourself. Every money count and your spending habits are the key to your financial recovery. Recognize the essentials; housing, food, utilities, and transportation focus on those first. This budget is your lifeline; it will guide you away from the pitfalls of financial chaos.

Now, let's talk about creating a surplus. Even if it's modest, having a surplus is critical. It becomes your buffer against unexpected expenses that could otherwise derail your progress. As you allocate funds, prioritize survival and stability. It's about building a safety net, brick by brick, even in the face of adversity.

Consider your income as a dynamic entity. Explore opportunities for additional earnings, whether through a second job, freelancing, or acquiring new skills. You have the power to improve your financial situation and every effort you make counts. Think of it as an investment in your future.

Looking beyond the immediate challenges, set long-term goals. Speak to yourself with conviction; affirm that you are not just surviving but building a future. This financial plan is your blueprint for a life filled with stability and happiness. Set achievable milestones; saving for education, acquiring property, or investing in skills that align with your aspirations.

In the absence of familial support, seek guidance from community resources or financial counselors. You may be alone, but you are not without resources. These experts can provide insights that will fortify your financial plan. Reach out, ask questions, and let their expertise complement your journey.

Embrace the challenges ahead with unwavering commitment. Remember, you are not merely surviving; you are thriving. Speak directly to yourself, affirm your capacity to shape your destiny, and through diligent financial planning, sculpt a path toward the happiness and security you truly deserve.

As you embark on this financial journey, remember that the power to shape your destiny lies within you. Through resilience, determination, and strategic financial planning, you can navigate the abyss and emerge on the other side with a life filled with promise and fulfillment.

7. Embrace Resilience

In the face of profound adversity, it is paramount to embrace resilience as a guiding force. Life's challenges may seem insurmountable, especially for someone who has lost family, lacked formal education, and possessed no apparent advantages. Yet, resilience is not a distant trait; it is a skill that can be cultivated, shaping a path toward a future filled with solutions and happiness.

Let's start by acknowledging the pain and grief that accompanies loss. Speak to yourself with kindness, recognizing the weight of the challenges while affirming your strength. Direct speech becomes a daily affirmation: I am facing immense challenges, but I am resilient. I have the power to shape my destiny and build a better future.

Resilience is not about denying reality but reframing it. Address the absence of formal education and tangible assets by focusing on intrinsic qualities. Speak to yourself about your potential and adaptability: I may lack a formal education, but I am resourceful and can learn. I may not have properties, but I possess the resilience to create a future of abundance.

Set tangible goals and cultivate a sense of purpose. Direct speech becomes a roadmap: I may not have a support system, but I can create one by connecting with like-minded individuals. I may lack special talents, but I can develop skills through dedication and practice. Resilience is nurtured through determination and a clear vision of the future.

Remember, resilience is not a solitary journey. Connect with those who have faced similar challenges; seek mentors and role models. Express your willingness to learn and grow: I am open to guidance and learning from those who have overcome adversity. I am not alone in my struggles, and there is strength in the community.

Celebrate small victories along the way. Remind yourself of challenges conquered, fostering a mindset of strength and determination. Speak to yourself about your resilience: I have faced difficulties before, and I have overcome them. Each challenge is an opportunity for growth, and I am becoming stronger with every step.

In conclusion, the journey toward a brighter future begins with the acknowledgment of one's resilience. Through direct speech, foster a mindset of strength, determination, and hope. Despite the hardships, a fulfilling and happy life is within reach. Embrace resilience as a companion on this transformative journey, shaping a narrative of triumph over adversity.

8. Health and Wellness

In the face of adversity, it's essential to recognize the profound impact that taking care of both your physical and mental health can have on your journey toward a brighter future. Let's explore practical strategies together as if I were sitting with you, offering guidance on how to prioritize your well-being during challenging times.

9. Physical Health

Begin by crafting a daily routine that incorporates healthy habits. Picture this: "I know it's tough, but try to establish a daily routine. It doesn't have to be rigid, but having a routine can bring a sense of order to your life. In what you do, include regular meal times, ensuring your plate boasts a colorful array of fruits, vegetables, lean proteins, and whole grains. Eating well may seem like a small thing, but it can make a big difference. Try to include a variety of foods in your meals, and don't forget to drink enough water.

Now, let's talk about movement, engage in physical activities that bring you joy, whether it's a brisk walk, yoga, or simple home workouts. As I speak directly to you: Even a short walk or a few minutes of stretching can do wonders. Find an activity that you like, and try to incorporate it into your routine. And remember, prioritize sleep as a cornerstone of your well-being. Create a bedtime routine that signals your body it's time to wind down.

In 2016, I underwent surgery for endometriosis and experienced persistent lower back pain afterward. Realizing the potential benefits of exercise in my recovery, I decided to incorporate various physical activities into my routine. I started with walking, jogging, hiking, and occasionally going to the gym for additional exercises. These activities significantly contributed to the improvement of my back pain, and today, I am fit and capable of performing my daily tasks without any issues, especially running around with the children I teach in nursery school.

10. Mental Health

Recognize that seeking support is not a sign of weakness but a courageous step towards healing. In my direct speech to you; It's okay to ask for help. Talk to someone you trust, whether it's a friend, a family member, or a professional. You don't have to face everything alone. Incorporate mindfulness practices, such as meditation or deep breathing exercises, into your daily routine. These techniques can help you stay grounded and manage stress. Mindfulness can be a lifeline during tough times. Take a few minutes each day to focus on your breath or engage in activities that bring you peace.

Set realistic goals, breaking down larger aspirations into smaller, achievable tasks. As I encourage you directly: It might seem daunting to think about the future right now. Break down your goals into smaller steps. Each step forward is a victory. Surround yourself with positive influence, whether it's uplifting music, inspirational quotes, or engaging in activities that bring you joy. Find small sources of joy and hold onto them. It could be music, a hobby, or simply spending time in nature. Positivity can be a powerful force.

In conclusion, remember that nurturing your physical and mental health is a gradual process. Picture each piece of advice as a stepping stone on your journey toward a future filled with solutions and happiness. It's okay to ask for help, prioritize your health, and celebrate the victories, no matter how small. You're not alone on this path and your well-being matters.

11. Explore Passion and Hobbies

In the face of overwhelming challenges, my advice to you, dear reader, is to explore passion and hobbies as a powerful tool to overcome hard times and carve a path toward a brighter future. Life's adversities, such as the loss of family, not having access for a better education, and lack of support, necessitate a transformative approach;

one that begins with the identification of your interests.

Take a moment for introspection. What activities bring you joy, curiosity, or a sense of accomplishment? Whether it's painting, writing, playing a musical instrument, gardening, coding, or any other pursuit, the key is to find something that resonates with you on a personal level.

This isn't about achieving perfection; it's about relishing the journey and the learning experience it brings.

Once you've identified your passions, immerse yourself fully in these activities. Dedicate time regularly to explore and develop them, letting them become a positive outlet for your emotions and stress. Establish a routine, create structure in your life, and build discipline and focus through the pursuit of what brings you fulfillment.

Consider this not merely a leisurely endeavor, but a journey of skill development. Even without a high-level education background, you can acquire practical and valuable skills through hands-on experiences in your chosen hobbies. This opens up new avenues for personal and professional growth that you might not have considered before.

Speaking of educational opportunities, it's essential not to overlook any chance to learn something new in life. In my case, despite having a background in accounting from high school, after I moved to Germany, I seized the opportunity to learn the German language and acquire skills in the education field. Now, I am a teacher at a school for young children, particularly those in nursery school. I find immense satisfaction and joy in my job, and the bond I share with my students is mutual; they love me, and I love them. It's a fulfilling experience that highlights the importance of embracing opportunities for personal and professional growth.

The social aspect of hobbies should not be overlooked. Join clubs, online communities, or local groups centered around your interests. Connecting with like-minded individuals not only provides a support network but can also offer guidance and encouragement during challenging times. Remember, you are not alone on this journey.

As your skills develop and your confidence grows, view your passions as a potential gateway to entrepreneurship. Whether you sell handmade crafts, offer services related to your hobby, or explore freelance opportunities, you can gradually build a foundation for financial stability on your terms.

In addition to that, understand that engaging in passion and hobbies is a form of self-care. Amidst life's difficulties, these activities offer moments of respite. The creative and fulfilling nature of your pursuits can positively impact your mental health, fostering a sense of purpose and reducing feelings of isolation.

The journey to overcoming hard times involves embracing the transformative power of passion and hobbies. By dedicating time to explore and nurture your interests, you can discover a sense of purpose, develop new skills, build a support network, and create opportunities for personal and professional growth. Through the pursuit of what brings you joy and fulfillment, you pave the way for a future filled with solutions, resilience, and happiness.

12. Community Resources

In the face of daunting challenges, it's crucial to recognize that community resources can be the key to unlocking a path toward a brighter future. Let me share some advice on how to navigate these turbulent times, drawing strength from the support networks that surround you.

When reaching out to local organizations and nonprofits, don't hesitate to speak directly about your needs and aspirations. Make those connections count by stating, I've faced immense hardships, losing my family and lacking a formal education. I am eager to turn my life around, and I believe your organization's resources could be instrumental in helping me achieve that. This direct approach can pave the way for tailored guidance and assistance.

Government agencies are often equipped with welfare programs, counseling services, and employment assistance initiatives. By scheduling meetings and engaging with social workers or case managers, you can articulate your situation with a statement like, I've experienced significant loss and am seeking support to rebuild my life. Can you guide me through the resources available within the community?

Religious institutions can also provide a supportive network. Attend services and engage with the community by stating your needs directly: I've faced profound loss and am seeking support to rebuild my life. Can you guide me to resources within the community or offer any assistance through your network? This open dialogue can lead to unexpected ways of help.

Education is a powerful tool for transformation. Even without a high-level education background, express your eagerness to learn and improve your skills: I may not have a formal education, but I am eager to learn and enhance my employability. Can you direct me to resources or programs that can help me gain knowledge? Libraries, adult education centers, and online platforms can offer valuable growth opportunities.

Networking within the community is equally crucial. Attend local events, join clubs, and express your story directly to others: I've faced immense challenges, and I'm actively seeking opportunities to connect with and contribute to the community. Can you suggest any local groups or events where I can make meaningful connections? Building relationships can lead to unforeseen support and collaboration.

Proactive engagement, clear communication, and having the will power to explore various possibilities is key to finding and utilizing community resources. Embrace the support and opportunities available within the community to overcome Any challenges and build a foundation for a better future. Your journey may be challenging, but with the help of those around you, it can become a transformative experience.

13. Learn from Role Models

In the pursuit of a brighter future amid challenging circumstances, learning from role models can be a transformative strategy. It begins with the identification of Right individuals who have triumphed over adversity. Look to those whose stories resonate with your challenges, be it in business, sports, science, or personal circles. These role models serve as guiding lights, demonstrating that success is achievable even in the face of seemingly insurmountable obstacles.

Once, you have pinpointed potential role models, dive into their life stories. Immerse yourself in biographies, documentaries, and interviews where they share their experiences.

This exploration is not just a passive endeavor; it's a journey to understand the struggles they faced, the setbacks they overcame, and the strategies they used to achieve success. Through this process, you will gain valuable insights, realizing that every successful individual, regardless of background, has confronted and conquered challenges.

From these narratives, extract life lessons that resonate with your circumstances. These lessons could encompass resilience, perseverance, adaptability and the importance of continuous learning. The goal is to distill the wisdom embedded in their journeys and apply it to your own life, laying the groundwork for personal development and growth.

Identifying traits in your role models that you admire is a crucial step. Whether it is their work ethic, determination, optimism, or interpersonal skills, these positive traits can become a foundation for your development. Emulate them consciously, integrating these qualities into your daily life to propel yourself forward.

Drawing inspiration from your role models, set realistic and achievable goals for yourself. Break down your aspirations into manageable steps, mirroring the journey of those who have walked a similar path. This step-by-step approach allows you to make progress gradually, moving closer to the positive and fulfilling life you envision.

Beyond the stories and lessons, seek out mentoring opportunities. While direct familial support may be absent, there are often avenues to connect with mentors who can provide guidance based on their experiences. Explore online platforms, networking events, or mentorship programs to find individuals willing to share their insights and support your journey.

Cultivate a growth mindset, an attitude that sees challenges as opportunities for development. Embrace the idea that abilities and intelligence can be nurtured through dedication and hard work. This mindset empowers you to persevere in the face of adversity, viewing challenges not as roadblocks but as stepping stones toward personal and professional growth.

Building a supportive network is essential. While your immediate family might not be present, connect with like-minded individuals who share similar aspirations. Attend community events, join online forums, or participate in workshops to build relationships with people who understand your journey and can provide encouragement.

Continuous learning is a cornerstone of success. Stay curious and invest time in acquiring new skills and knowledge. Adaptability to change is equally crucial. Be open to pivoting in the face of challenges, recognizing that flexibility is a key aspect of long-term success.

Lastly, celebrate your achievements, no matter how small. Each step toward your goals is a victory. Acknowledge and revel in these milestones to maintain motivation and momentum on your journey toward a brighter and happier future. Remember, even in the absence of immediate support, the stories of others can illuminate the path ahead.

14. What has helped me personally to find a way in my professional growth

In the darkest moments of my life, I found comfort and strength through a combination of therapy, support groups, and the power of sharing my story. My journey through adversity, spanning the horrors of the genocide against the Tutsi in 1994, the discrimination faced in Germany, and the challenges of divorce, led me to seek help and ultimately find resilience within myself.

The therapy courses at Konstanz University became a cornerstone in my healing process. Through these sessions, I was able to confront the pain and trauma that lingered from the genocide, discrimination and the dissolution of my marriage. The direct conversations with my therapist were like a lifeline, offering insights and coping mechanisms that gradually guided me toward a path of recovery.

Empowered by the knowledge gained from the therapy courses, I embarked on the transformative journey of writing my first book, "A Broken Life." It became a therapeutic outlet, allowing me to articulate and process the complex emotions that had weighed me down for so long. The act of writing not only helped me make sense of my experiences but also provided a source of strength that I could share with others facing their struggles.

Caritas Waldshut-Tiengen played a pivotal role in my healing process. Their counseling services provided a safe space for me to explore my emotions and confront the challenges I faced. In addition, their financial support enabled me to release and publish my book, amplifying the impact of my story and reaching a wider audience.

The Frauenreise group, where women gathered once a month to share their stories, became a sanctuary of understanding and empathy. As I recounted the harrowing loss of almost all my family members during the genocide, the other women, each carrying their burdens, listened with open hearts. My narrative served as a powerful catalyst for healing within the group.

Despite their pain, they found inspiration in my resilience, recognizing the strength and courage it took to overcome such profound challenges. In turn, this realization ignited a collective healing process among the women, fostering a sense of camaraderie and strength in the face of adversity.

Through therapy, the support of Caritas Waldshut-Tiengen, and the Frauenreise group, I discovered that sharing my story not only helped me heal but also became a source of inspiration and strength for others. In opening up about my experiences, I unintentionally created a ripple effect of healing and empowerment, proving that even in the darkest moments, the power of shared humanity can be an inspiration of light.

POEM TO MY MOM

Dear Mom,

In 1994, a year that brought so much sorrow,
You left, but your love still guides tomorrow.
At eleven, I felt a little bit lost,
But your teachings stayed, no matter the cost.

Those talks we had, just you and me,
Your advice, a treasure, so precious, you see.
Life got hard, and it was a bit scary,
But your words became my sanctuary.

As a teenager, oh, the choices to make,
Your wisdom led me, no room for mistakes.
I stuck to your words, even in the strife,
Guided by your lessons, shaping my life.

Now, I'm a mom and a happy wife too,
All thanks to the guidance that came from you.
I wish you could see the family I've made,
With love and joy, a story well begun.

Proudly your daughter, strong and true,

Your teachings in my heart, forever in view.
In every success, in every little story,
You're the wind beneath my sail.

61

Mom, you're in my thoughts, always nearby,
Your love and wisdom, oh, so clear.
Until we meet again, on that distant shore,
Thank you, Mom, I love you forevermore.

With heartfelt thanks,

Judence Kayitesi

ACKNOWLEDGEMENT

I would like to thank my editor Caissy Christine Nakure and cover designer Emile Tuyubahe and layout designer Andreas Schäfer for dedicating their time and creativity to this book.

Special thanks to Divine Gashugi for the forewords and for empowering me to keep moving onto the second book and to Thomas Mazimpaka for advice on this book and all support in my writing.

I would like to thank Laurette Annely Akariza for proofreading and all support on this book and Inzozi Publisher Team for your support.

Lastly but most importantly, thanks to my partner and my Children for the love and ability to tolerate my mood and absence.

REFERENCES

I would like to express gratitude to various sources that contributed to the research and inspiration for this book. I want to thank the wealth of information gathered through online research, including search engines such as Google, which provided valuable insights into the broader context of the themes explored in "Choosing Resilience, Unlocking the Rhythm of the Human Spirit."

Walls, J. (2005). The Glass Castle. Scribner.

Westover, T. (2018). Educated. Random House.

Peck, M. S. (1978). The Road Less Traveled. Simon & Schuster.

Strayed, C. (2012). Wild: From Lost to Found on the Pacific Crest Trail. Alfred A. Knopf.

Frankl, V. E. (1946). Man's Search for Meaning. Beacon Press.

McBride, J. (1996). The Color of Water: A Black Man's Tribute to His White Mother. Riverhead Books.

Kristof, N. D., & WuDunn, S. (2009). Half the Sky: Turning Oppression into Opportunity for Women Worldwide. Vintage.

Vance, J. D. (2016). Hillbilly Elegy: A Memoir of a Family and Culture in Crisis. Harper.

Skloot, R. (2010). The Immortal Life of Henrietta Lacks. Crown Publishing Group.

Kalanithi, P. (2016). When Breath Becomes Air. Random House